ANYONE CAN BE SUCCESSFUL

ANYONE CAN BE SUCCESSFUL

Come Inside and Find Out How . . .

BEN OXFORD

Copyright © 2015 by Ben Oxford.

Library of Congress Control Number: 2015902141
ISBN: Hardcover 978-1-5035-0272-7
Softcover 978-1-5035-0271-0
eBook 978-1-5035-0273-4

All rights reserved. No part of this book may be reproduced or transmitted in any form or by any means, electronic or mechanical, including photocopying, recording, or by any information storage and retrieval system, without permission in writing from the copyright owner.

Any people depicted in stock imagery provided by Thinkstock are models, and such images are being used for illustrative purposes only.
Certain stock imagery © Thinkstock.

Print information available on the last page.

Rev. date: 02/10/2015

To order additional copies of this book, contact:
Xlibris
1-800-455-039
www.Xlibris.com.au
Orders@Xlibris.com.au

CONTENTS

Preface 7
Acknowledgements 11

Chapter 1: Let's get to know how we can control
our own brain and make a positive change!............... 13
Chapter 2: Managing and Understanding Self-Esteem 18
Chapter 3: How do we start reprogramming and programming
our control centre for a much better life and for
great success, let's stop talking about it and get on
with some simple—however, effective—strategies! 23
Chapter 4: Communication is the Essence of Success 28
Chapter 5: Managing Difficult Behaviours
for Conflict Resolution 39
Chapter 6: Goal Setting and Navigating Our Path for Success.... 47
Chapter 7: Feedback and Mirroring:
Adapting our Behaviour for Success 51
Chapter 8: Professional Athlete Approach to our Well-Being 55

Conclusion 67
Author Biography 69
Index 73

Preface

Did you know the brain thinks approximately five hundred words per minute? It has been scientifically proven that most of what we think is negative and has been born from the belief that survival instincts motivate this. If we were living in caveman days skipping and singing along and patting and smiling at dinosaurs, we may not have survived as long as we have without having critical and or negative thoughts in the blend.

Today, with the pressures of money, job, and career competition, population explosion globally, increased competition, exposure of personal publicity with social media, being time-poor, busy lives, breaking down of global borders, variations on traditional family constructs and distances conquered 'one world', introducing neighbours from so many diverse cultures, religions, belief systems, and complexities, it challenges us 'mere mortal humans' to stay positive and resilient against these pressures, for example, 'Where do I belong?' or 'Why is difference a disadvantage?'

Yes, you are. Normal pressures do exist; you don't have to 'Build a bridge', 'Take a cup of concrete to toughen up', 'Be a man', 'Be a lady', 'Toughen up, princess', or 'Stop being weak, too emotional'. *You are normal*, and this handbook will help you to understand the most important asset in your entire life. This asset you own will take you through your whole life and will determine your ultimate destiny. If you think of a wonderful house and home or a great motor vehicle that has stood the test of time and needed servicing along the way and a few upgrades, then this may help with understanding what we are up to . . .

This is about . . . **you. Yes, you—heart, head, body, and soul!**

People may say, 'But he does not know me? How can he help me to enable great success and determine my destiny?' Well, we have differences as human beings; however, we also have a lot of commonalities, and it is these commonalities I will focus on—for example, do you ever get cold? Do you ever feel hot? Do you ever get hungry? Do you get tired? Do you laugh at something that was funny? Do you ever have negative thoughts? Good, it is because you and me, we are human!

Of course there are exceptions to any rule so to speak, and if someone sadly has a severe and profound disability that hinders the standard functions, then this handbook may only partly apply. Here we go—practical enabling tools for surviving and conquering yesterday (reprogramming), today (designing), and tomorrow (delivering and exceeding expectations).

This handbook will be your best friend. People always remember how you made them feel, not so much what you say or do, so it will be tough as this is a book. My goal is to ensure that the reader gets some of the benefit that I have had in using this as a guide, and when put into practice, seeing and feeling the benefits will allow me to again achieve something I believed in and wanted to do as well. Through helping myself, I can now help the many.

This positive formula works in most cases against all we are told we are, should be, or will be. We will be who we want to be no matter what our background, race, gender, looks, sexual preference, socio-economic status, or other human derivation that could potentially stereotype us from others; however, we will not allow us to stereotype ourselves! Stereotypes are often caused through personality inadequacies of the person throwing the insult, opinion, or comment; for example, an overweight person will often be the first to criticize an overweight person. What people don't like about themselves is often what they cast upon others!

It can be hard to know what or who we are. Or where we belong. Or even why others have had better start-up lives than us—a silver spoon in their mouths.

This handbook has been written by a survivor of life and a conqueror of life coming from adversity, harm, anger, and sadness. I turned this around by stopping listening to those that were set up in my life as the most influential such as some teachers, bosses, some family members, and introduced 'friends'.

Through self-belief (yes, it sounds cliché), however, it will explain how we enable this and understand the way we can determine, change, and lead positively wonderful lives against what feels like it is against all odds (sometimes) and deliver the opposite of what most people tell us we were or will be and also what we should believe in and how we should behave. For example, you should be humble and give to others. Duty before self—money does not matter, and similar.

These are wonderful ideals; however, if you do not put yourself first and set your own happiness and health up, then you are no good to others. Believe in yourself, and others will believe in you. If it is to be, it is up to me. WIFM—what is in it for me? Once this is cemented, you can do anything, absolutely anything, and I have done (almost) everything and achieved (almost) every goal I ever wanted to achieve and also helped millions in the process, and through the methods in this book, I am a self-made millionaire financially and coming from nothing financially.

The areas I have worked in or led in throughout my career have all been awarded independently at state, national, and international levels for excellence, and not bad for someone that was told he was dumb and did poorly at school and could not get into higher education. I ended up with three degrees from three different universities with Distinction averages and, yes, scored some As at master's level) and carried out these studies while working full-time. Every personal goal I have ever set has been achieved to date.

Now strap yourself in as we go on the ride of our life—no one can stop you now! ***Go for gold,*** and I am excited to be able to share some of this with you!

Acknowledgements

I would like to especially note some inspirational knowledge I have drawn through my own studies and experiences in creating this one-stop-shop book of success: literature reviews and over a decade of academic studies in communications at the Northern Territory University (now Charles Darwin University) during my bachelor's in teaching (adult and vocational), Murdoch University during my postgraduate studies in Bachelor of Professional Studies, Edith Cowan University during my postgraduate studies for a master's in education (major in leadership). Other programs that I have taught and used over my career are Allan Pease, Dr Patricia Cameron Hill, *The Secret*, Job Club program, DARE program, studies at the Northern Territory Police Service, professional supervision studies, Prof. Mike and Dr Brenda Clare, University of Western Australia, Crucial Conversations Training, and over twenty years as a senior leader and executive manager across most sectors—private, public, and non-profit.

I would also like to thank the following for their proofreading and support:

Chris Lejmanoski (chairman, Customer Service Council of Australia)
Janice Bodman (human resource and customer service professional)
Josephine Oxford (my mother and finance and customer service professional)
Maureen Dakers (information and communication technology and customer service professional)

Special thanks to:

Jason Chatfield (professional internationally recognized illustrator)

Chapter 1

Let's get to know how we can control our own brain and make a positive change!

*Repeated Believed—Subconscious—Belief System—World View;
Ignored Messages—Conscious—Deflected—Not Absorbed*

The human brain is often not understood, and once you understand your own brain, what the conscious and subconscious means, the creation of one's current situation and future destiny through the power of the brain, and the design of what you are and can change into is a phenomenally powerful and essential tool to being successful, as a hammer is to a nail.

The brain is like a muscle, and those that have ever exercised strenuously know the pain as the muscles are conditioned and the effort needed to build muscle and maintain a level of fitness. The brain is no different. If you think of the brain as a muscle—no pain, no gain—the more we force ourselves to learn new things, even things we don't really want to learn or do, the brain grows, as does our intelligence and ability to cope. For example, the more we learn, the bigger the brain grows and the more 'folds' we get on our brain like a ripped abs, bulging biceps, or a toned stomach. These folds are often related to the cognition of our brain (intelligence), and as this grows, often people refer to metacognition (we understand our own intelligence and thinking), which is the awareness of oneself and one's learning and actions.

Without complicating this chapter too much, in essence the conscious brain is what happens day to day—we see, smell, and think things, and often it is routine. The subconscious brain is the things that we have stored and learnt in the past and stored as our belief system, often not aware this is happening. The key here is to ensure what we store makes us a better person strengthening our soul, body, well being and happiness.

If we continually absorb negative feedback and we believe this, this will become our destiny. If we recognize negative feedback and identify it when it is coming and ensure we don't believe it, then it will not be stored in our subconscious and hence won't influence the way we behave and the person we become.

The human brain is very similar to a computer program; we are in control of what we want to program for our lives! The brain is the control centre that informs us of what we are, where we are going, and how we are going to get there and ultimately gets us there and allows us to go further!

Understanding how we can control our brain, the way we absorb knowledge through the conscious world creates our destiny through the subconscious, and the stored messages are integral to success and quite easy to master. Throughout this book, there will be key themes on how we do this.

How we can program who we are or debug the current program and reprogram who we are and what we want to be and make our dreams come true through this process of understanding what we are doing to our control centre (brain), or more importantly, what other people are doing to our control centre (brain), belief system, and ultimately, who we believe we are and the messages that are getting in the way of who we really want to be.

This can be harder for some, especially when redesigning our DNA or belief system of who we are and what we are capable of. This is especially in the formative years from zero to seven years old; this is where the human brain has the most physical growth and, in essence, the most influence on our belief system. So understandably, we are naive and would not be able to be expected to know how to operate and control our own control centre—the brain. This can be a harmful period in general as a young person growing up; the most influential people at this time whom we believe in and who send the messages that we end up storing ultimately become the constructs of who we believe we are and set our capabilities most often based on what other people think of us for the future. This can be great if we are one of the lucky ones; however, most of us are not.

The biggest influencers are immediate people in the circle of life: family, teachers, friends, social groups and sporting groups, and social media and media in general. So if messages have been sent to you either through believing them or repetition, then they have begun to create who you are. Your brain muscle is 'working out' potentially in the wrong direction; your subconscious and belief system may not be aligned to your original dreams and belief systems. For example, you may want to be a good sports person, vet, millionaire, police officer, doctor, or executive in a high-rise and have a hot boyfriend or girlfriend. However, the messages sent to your control centre—the brain has told you that you are too weak, ugly, useless, not very bright, not as smart or as good as your brother or the kid next door, a dreamer and too lazy, uncoordinated, stupid, too childish, immature, loud, irresponsible, embarrassing, good at maths, a worrier—some of these key influencers especially as a young person and continuing through life affect the self-esteem dramatically, and we will talk more about the self-esteem and heart later in this book.

The brain can redesign who we are through a number of strategies, and you can align your control centre (brain) and the messages you take in and the goals to be achieved and will reap the benefits once mastered. This book will look at successful strategies for enhancing your control centre, the brain, and also, if appropriate, redesign the control centre and brain through the correct messages being absorbed and deflected, redirecting the wrong messages that are not aligned to the belief system and the current situation and successful future you want.

The reality is most of us are born equal; the human body and brain are incredibly resilient, adaptable, and immensely powerful. This book will try and untap your inner power, strength, and brain control to not only live a better life, but also allow you to see a marked change on your journey to success or enhance current successes!

Chapter 2

Managing and Understanding Self-Esteem

Self-esteem is our evaluation, emotions, judgment, and attitude of our own worth. Our worth is assessed by what we believe and store in our subconscious control centre (brain), which creates our own world view and also what we believe is our own competency. This belief of one's self is influenced directly by our life experiences and control centre constructs (brain). This self-belief is created in real time and the cumulative effect ultimately determines who and what we are today and our destiny. This is a very high-maintenance part of our existence and can be hard to sustain if we do not understand how it gets affected, manipulated by external forces such as other people, environment, and situations we are placed in either voluntarily (social, work) or compulsorily (family). The illustration in this chapter is a helpful tool in understanding how our self-esteem can affect our overall well-being and health.

Ultimately, self-esteem is referred to in a lot of cases as the heart; you may have heard the terminology 'head and heart' due to the self-esteem being directly related to our emotions. The fact is the heart and emotions are still controlled by the control centre (brain). The brain has a component amongst others that controls our emotions and will be referred to later in this book.

You awaken in the morning feeling wonderful; a good night's sleep and a fresh day awaits. You get up and realize you have not ironed your shirt. You are walking from your car or the bus stop, and the weather changes quickly, and it begins to rain heavily; you get wet and now have to break into a jog to avoid being soaked and are annoyed as the weather report said rain was not due until the afternoon. As you are walking into work, a colleague laughs at you and rolls his/her eyes because you are wet and looking frustrated. As you get out of the lift and walk towards your office, a manager says in a loud voice, 'Hope you are putting a tie on. Did you forget?' then walks away. By the time you get to the office, you start to panic as you are not sure what you have forgotten. Checking the day's schedules, you have an external company visiting today and you need to be present. Now concerned about not wearing the correct clothes, you go now to get a coffee, and the coffee machine is not working. The boss walks in and starts complaining about the staff that work with you and is not happy and hard to please. Returning to your office, the phone rings, and your mother has been taken ill and has to go to the hospital. This has all occurred before lunchtime, and your self-esteem has taken a battering. So how do we ensure that we can sustain professionalism throughout the rest of the day and also bounce back for tomorrow and the rest of the week?

We need to be aware of what is happening to our emotional state and self-esteem. All that has to happen now is for a critical incident to occur at work—for example, the boss yells at you for failing to deliver on a task. A loved one dies and that's the end—nothing left to fight with or to run with in the day-to-day challenges of life—this is when people get run down, distressed (stress is a stimulus—it is good for us—however, prolonged and too much stress can cause an overload, distress), sick, and unwell.

So how do we ensure we have enough energy to also keep some in reserve to ensure we don't only survive the tougher days but also conquer these and continue with great happiness, health, and resilience, today, tomorrow, and onwards?

The strategy is always to drive, not be driven; lead, not follow; always have that petrol tank quarter full; and have 20 per cent of your healthy energy in reserve every day!

How do we do this well? What I do is I visualize a balloon fully inflated at the start of the day, and I recognize those things that hit my conscious world in a negative way, the things that change my posture, the self-talk shifts to the negative, allowing negative comments to chink the armour. When the energy drains, the stress starts to reach distress. So every time something happens, I picture some of the air being released from the balloon. As the air continually decreases and gets to the point where it is going to shrivel to a wilted piece of plastic on the ground, I find ways to not only prevent deflation but also ways to increase inflation and sustain a healthy balloon with enough air in it to breathe and walk confidently while still having enough energy, head and heart (yin and yang), to give back to the areas that should matter: work, family, friends, and self!

You awake in the morning feeling great after a good night's sleep, and if you were to picture a balloon, the scenario shared in this chapter can be applied. As each negative feedback is received, the balloon deflates, or it can work the other way where we reverse the process and inflate rather than deflate. In chapter 3, we specifically look at ways of shielding and absorbing, which in turn assist in inflating the balloon—your self-esteem remains inflated and your well-being improved.

It is also very important to engage in reflective practice—learn where things have not gone right and make the change. Put in the effort to find the time and discovery on how you can better preserve the inflated balloon and your overall well-being. Changing your patterns, routines, and behaviour through critical reflection and prior planning is essential. You may have heard of the term 'the six Ps'—it is, in my opinion, true! PPPPPP—prior preparation prevents piss-poor performance!

In the example given, some examples of critical reflection and prior planning to make the positive change are always have a spare ironed shirt and leave a tie hanging at work as required, have an umbrella close by, change your travel route to avoid negative people first thing in the morning, and apply chapter 4 to deal with poor communicators that are identified as deflating your balloon and wasting energy and time through deflection strategies.

To assist in understanding self-esteem and supporting positive inflation, a great exercise I have used over many years, age groups, and all walks of life and that works in group situations is you ask each person to write down something positive about what they think of each other, including you!

These compliments often surprise other people, and I know it has surprised me in the past in a very positive and rewarding way, as we often don't realize that there are some really great things that we do, say, or act on, and we need this recognition to support our control centre (brain) and overall well-being.

These compliments really increase your self-esteem, and I always recommend that the people keep these close by such as in their draw, on their desk, and from time to time, when the balloon (self-esteem) feels deflated, refer back to the list of compliments to remind you that you are OK and, in a lot of cases, better than OK. This also helps the control centre to remember the positives and absorb these at a time (or times) most needed.

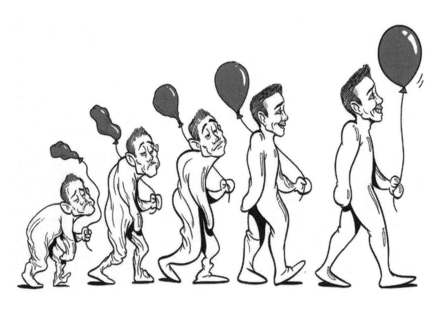

Chapter 3

How do we start reprogramming and programming our control centre for a much better life and for great success, let's stop talking about it and get on with some simple-however, effective-strategies!

The brain thinks approximately five hundred words per minute. We are in constant dialogue with ourselves; we only say approximately 178 words per minute. This dialogue has been proven to mostly be negative, originally born from the survival instinct of our ancestors. To control what words are being constantly bandied around, we need to understand what we want to take in and what we are also saying to ourselves to ensure we remain positive and align our control centre (brain) to the current and/or future destiny we want to have in our design of success and personal goals customized to our dreams, needs, and wants.

Feedback is very good for adapting our behaviour to the various situations and contexts that are presented to us; especially in a work environment, we often have to change our colours to suit the various roles and positions we take on—like a chameleon. The issue is where feedback is motivated for the wrong reasons and prolonged negative feedback that is absorbed can become stored messages and affect our well-being and self-esteem. In effect, this feedback can change what and where we want to be. In essence, feedback to adapt our behaviour in the positive is important; however, we do not want to change who we are and what we stand for, when others have agendas not aligned to our well-being.

An example could be a manipulative colleague or boss who is threatened by your abilities and wants to ensure that the good work, attitude, and position is not sustained for their own preservation and personal gain.

To ensure we are staying positive and our world view is aligned to what we want out of our lives, we need to recognize messages being sent to us that are not healthy and are not good for our self-esteem and well-being. To assist in recognizing these and blocking them, visualize a shield that deflects these negative unhealthy messages and flick these away.

When we receive constructive, healthy feedback, then we need to absorb these. The opposite of deflecting is absorbing. Picture these messages entering and remaining within ourselves and making us stronger. Accept compliments with a humble 'thank you'! The thank you is the trigger expression for absorption. Never deflect a compliment—these are great for building our self-esteem and positive constructs in the control centre (brain). Often people feel awkward when compliments are given; this is a natural reaction especially if we are not used to receiving these often or from someone who does not normally offer them. To prevent embarrassment and losing this valuable feedback, just say 'thank you'!

Repetition of these positive messages and compliments to support our inflation and self-esteem can be reinforced via strategies of visual aids (such as written-up lists, photos, pictures, letters, messages), also surrounding yourself around good people that often provide praise and wonderful feedback that support and help, as long as the intent is motivated by good will and is accurate (constructive versus destructive), helpful, and genuine. The repetition and being reminded regularly is very positive and supports the way your control centre (brain), body, and soul energize your self-perception, emotional status, and personal worth. Also, it provides an essential ingredient in the overall approach to your goal setting and success.

Positive Example

Compliment sent: 'Ben, you look very smart today. Is that a new suit?'
Response: 'Thanks, it is an oldie but a goodie, I do like it' (absorbed the compliment).

Negative Example

Compliment sent: 'Ben, you look very smart today. Is that a new suit?'
Response: 'This old thing? I have had it for years and doesn't fit as well as it used to. Wish I could afford a new suit.'

The repetition of messages we believe will be absorbed, so it is also very important not only to recognise the negative messages but also deflect them if they are repeated. If our resilience is down, we may absorb these without even knowing. So if we are in a situation where we have to work with a colleague or a family member that we have to see on a regular basis, then we must get our shields up and prepare to deflect and not absorb.

In some cases where our resilience is being pushed down and the messages are mostly negative, then there does come a time to make a step change and remove yourself from the situation and/or people that are sending these.

This is the last resort, however, in my career, where I have done everything possible and, at the end of the day, the personality conflict and constant attacks resulted in me leaving. This has also happened with some friends and family over my life. There comes a point where, no matter what you do for you and them, acknowledging the negative behaviour will bring you down. Thankfully this is the exception, not the norm.

Often people say to me I don't look old enough to be my age—'You don't have grey hair, etc. I believe this has come from ensuring the people I surround myself with are positive and supportive and the jobs I have done are what I want to do and are a part of my goal pathway and I am on the right frequency!

Recognizing and Shielding
Remember to flick it or keep it.

Chapter 4

Communication is the Essence of Success

Global statistics and multiple sources advise consistently that approximately 80 to 85 per cent of our success in life is directly attributable to our communication skills. This is above any academic qualifications, work, and life experience.

This chapter breaks communication skills into three crucial categories:

- voice communication
- non-voice communication and physical language
- action listening and paraphrasing

These three communication styles when used in collaboration will allow your conscious and subconscious messages to be in sync and enable successful personal and professional relationships to grow and enable success. People always remember how you made them feel (heart), not so much what you said.

Did you know that within the first few seconds of meeting someone, they subconsciously and instinctively judge you and, in a lot of cases, make up their minds whether they like or dislike you? This impression may not be what you consciously said; however, the non-voice and physical language messages you have sent without even knowing subconsciously ultimately can determine the judgment made and the success of the relationship.

Human beings do judge other human beings, and it may be the way you did or did not look at the person, your facial expression, head movements, style and depth of the handshake (weak or too strong), physical posture (stooped or proud), voice projection or the lack of it (can or cannot hear you), failure to exercise the communication triangle (lack of eye contact), the clothes you are wearing and their condition (crumpled or smart suit), the way you smell (pleasant or unclean, bad breath), and so much more.

Our image is our personal brand and tells others so much about us. The image we send will be judged on what others have experienced in their lives, so it is critical we understand how to make that great first impression as opposed to a forgettable and unpleasant experience. We only truly get one chance to make a great first impression!

Voice Communication

Voice communication can only work if the message being sent is heard, so projection and volume does matter; for example you may have heard the saying 'the squeaky wheel gets the oil!'

When speaking, the words need to be articulate, succinct, and avoid verbosity as the human brain thinks approximately five hundred words per minute—we only speak approximately 178—and to ensure the message is heard, you need a captive audience (encode the message = design and deliver the message). To ensure the message is understood, look for voice confirmation and feedback (decode the message = the receiver understands the message). for example, 'What do you think?' or 'Do you have an opinion?' Send the message to the receiver's communication triangle if looking outside the triangle of the eyes, nose, and mouth area. This will send a subconscious message that you are not focused, and also, they may not hear the verbal message clearly as the framing for the concentration has not been set.

To know that a person is listening to you, you need to observe eye contact. The ears only take in noise or sound; the eyes filter the information and concentrate on the subject matter at hand. It can and has been said that we actually listen with our eyes. We have all probably heard when growing up, 'Look at me when I am talking to you.' I remember at school, teachers would always say 'Eyes to the front.'

Eye contact is the way the human brain is able to absorb and decode (understand the message). While the brain turns over approximately five hundred words per minute, voice messaging only sends approximately 178 words, so to ensure clarity in the message, eye contact is so incredibly important. As soon as the eyes look away, all other thoughts and words pour in, and the concentration is lost.

See below cartoon illustration by Jason as an example.

Voice communication needs to keep the receiver of the message interested to ensure they get the message, understand the message, and of course, use the message to enable their original purpose for the message.

The delivery of the message needs good reason and intelligence around the content of the message (not just talking for the sake of it, waffle); for example, key areas for potency and effectiveness should include

- fluctuation of tone,
- sincerity,
- empathy,
- clear articulation of the words being used,
- belief,
- enthusiasm, and
- energy in what is being said and delivered to the recipient.

In some cases where the communication is critical, you may need to visualize the person as a best friend, loved one, or family member so the empathy is genuine and felt.

Remember people always remember how you made them feel, not what you generally said.

To make a person feel what you are saying, you need to find a common ground and interest and go on a discovery of what is of (heart) interest to them. Create a personal professional relationship.

For example, WIFM (what's in it for me?) is common human behaviour; once a common ground is established, the relationship can grow. This may be something such as family or children; a common acquaintance; a football club; pets; place of birth; clothing brands; boating, fishing, or sporting teams; nationality; age; social interests; and/or job types.

Weave a common ground into the communication conversation, and their subconscious will trigger an emotional connection to you. They may not even be aware why they like you; it will be the common discovery ground and emotional connection.

For example, when you first meet people in your life, you may walk away from someone and either think to yourself or voice to a friend or colleague, 'I don't know why, I just don't like him/her' or 'There is something about that person I just don't trust.' This, as we are uncovering in this book, could simply be the way they did or did not look at you, their posture, or lack of good communication skills in general.

On the other hand, you will, in your life, after first meeting someone, walk away and say, 'I really like that person, I don't know why—she/he seems really cool and nice.' For the most part, this is because that person has been able to trigger a personal emotional connection with you and has established a common ground of discovery.

WE LISTEN AND FOCUS WITH OUR EYES.

THE BRAIN THINKS 500 WORDS PER MINUTE. WE ONLY SPEAK AROUND 178 WORDS PER MINUTE.

Non-Voice Communication and Physical Language

Non-voice communication is different from physical language although closely related. Physical language is overt and physical, such as obvious arm crossing and/or posture. Non-voice communication is often subconscious. An example of how voice communication can be contradicted by non-voice communication is when we are saying one thing with our mouths—'Yes, I agree totally, and I am happy with the decision'—however, the eyes are looking away (not listening or believing), the head is shaking from left to right (saying no instead of yes), and our arms are folded in a defensive position (protecting the vital organs such as the heart).

Another example is where a person will say 'I don't care,' yet they look downwards at their heart, which is a non-voice signal that they do care. When a person looks up to the left and/or right, they are remembering (left, truthful) or creating (right, making up) their messaging.

When trained in non-voice or physical language, the power of the subconscious messaging far outweighs the obvious voice messaging (conscious).

Anyone that has been trained in communication skills, especially advanced communication skills, will identify immediately that the words are not aligned to the non-voice communication messages being sent. It is critical that the verbal messaging matches what we are saying with our non-voice and physical language communication. This can occur more often in stressful situations and controlled environments; this is when we are most at risk of sending contradictory messaging.

This book will support you in recognizing and adapting our behaviour and communication styles through enablers outlined, especially through the control centre (brain) functions.

In the first few seconds of meeting someone, as previously discussed, they will judge you. To make a good first impression, we need to have good posture (shoulders back, standing up straight). Leaning into the handshake means you are interested in the subject matter at hand. A nice firm handshake says you are confident and interested as opposed to a soft, weak, limp handshake, which means you are not interested and may have low self-esteem and confidence in yourself. The polar opposite is the handshake that is too hard; this can indicate arrogance or being overbearing, overconfident, and even intimidating, depending on the person being introduced.

Non-voice communication includes personal hygiene, bad breath, or body odour; too much perfume or aftershave can be as equally off-putting as body odour.

We need to have self-awareness, and if in doubt, never be afraid to ask for constructive feedback from your support system.

A support system is essential in helping us to understand more about ourselves. Constructive feedback is essential in helping us to adapt our behaviour for success without losing our identity. The key to a successful support system is the people in this group need to be trusted, and you need to feel safe in their company and have a level of belief in their ability to help you through challenging times and, most importantly, that they are there when you reach out and need them. Their intent for your well-being has to be real and genuine (no hidden agendas).

Healthy support systems are usually made up of trusted family members, friends, colleagues, neighbours, role models, and coaches such as superiors at work; professionals such as psychologists or teachers; and people you look up to, admire, and most of all, respect. Support systems may only include two or three people but, as we get older, expand to up to a dozen.

Action Listening

Listening, as we have recently discovered, does not only include the obvious, our ears taking in sound and noise, but also the crucial component of our eyes and eye contact in the communication triangle (eyes, nose, mouth area). We have also recently discovered that voice communication, non-voice communication, and physical language also play a major integrated role in how we communicate. The same elements apply to action listening.

With action listening, we need to paraphrase in long conversations (not too much or it will be seen as a distraction). However, paraphrasing is a really good voice tool for active listening that reminds the person/people speaking to you that not only are you listening but you are also engaged as you are feeding back (decoding = understanding) the information being sent to you (encoding designed message).

For example, this is a message being sent (encode-designing): 'The budget is tracking to success year to date, and we are going to get a good return on investment as the outcome by the end of this financial year.' Here is the paraphrased feedback: 'Great news, sounds like a positive budget is in order.' This feedback is a crucial element of active listening and allows a good two-way approach. This sends a positive and encouraging conscious and subconscious reinforcement that you are interested in the person and subject matter at hand.

Action listening also includes positive reinforcement; this is where we send positive verbal feedback at various intervals such as 'aha', 'mmm', 'yes, good', 'I get it', and nodding our heads gently in the affirmative while leaning forward towards the person/people sending the message while maintaining eye contact in their communication triangle.

The above example has our three communication skills choreographed into an orchestra of action listening.

Communication channels need to send the same aligned, believable two-way messages.

Chapter 5

Managing Difficult Behaviours for Conflict Resolution

When we are put in a confrontationist or poor behaviour-management situation with another, we have a choice of how we respond, depending on what the desired outcome is. For example, is it managing upwards with a difficult boss when you want to retain your role and further enhance your career? Is it a difficult work colleague? school friend? family member? No matter what the situation, if we buy some time, even a few seconds, and recognize the traits of a potential attack, approach, conflict, or uncomfortable situation, then we adapt to one of the three modes of behaviour and communication. We can avoid conflict, change another's behaviour towards us, and achieve our goals through understanding how someone may be behaving towards us and how we can take control to ensure we are being communicated with in a respectful and safe way. The understanding of the alpha, equal, and submissive styles will then allow us to recognize our own behaviour and how others are behaving towards us. The key here is to know when to change gears and shift into one of the three modes of operation to ensure a positive and desired outcome is achieved. As we progress through this chapter, we will discover the meaning of these styles and how we can use these modes of operation to change other people's behaviours towards us as well.

Often, we are placed in difficult situations where the pressure is being put upon us, and it may be in a confronting and aggressive way. We naturally respond in an immediate emotional way as a natural defence mechanism. Our body releases adrenaline, posture stiffens, throat tightens, and the heart pumps faster to circulate essential defensive organs and parts of the body. Our heart rate increasing also sends blood from the frontal part of our brain (where rationale reasoning and calculated decision-making takes place) to the rear side of the brain (where our emotions are run). It is often referred to as a fight-or-flight reaction, caged-tiger syndrome, and similar terms.

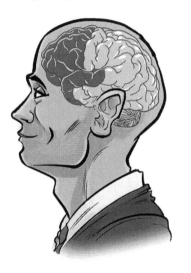

In essence, this is how we prepare to defend ourselves as a natural reaction. This may have been appropriate when fighting an enemy for survival in a primitive time; however, in the modern age and civilized world, in artificial environments such as offices, classrooms, or similar, this is not appropriate.

It is important that when someone has made you upset, angry, or mad that we immediately identify these characteristics (raised voice, unfair comments, offensive behaviour such as finger pointing, angry demeanour) and buy some time, even a few seconds, so we can prepare our response and the behaviour style we will adapt to diffuse and resolve the situation there and then and allow the door to remain open, so to speak, if we want to come back and fix it at a later date without burning any bridges. Taking a break—'engage brain before mouth', 'take a gap', 'time out', and 'don't say something you may regret' would be familiar terms that you may have heard of previously. By taking a break (even a few seconds/minutes), it allows the blood to return to the decision-making part of the brain (as you have calmed down) and further gives you some more time to work through reasoning on how you may be able to manage the awkward and possibly harmful situation you are in.

Taking the space/break or time out prior to responding will further give you time to engage the appropriate demeanour and/or behaviour based on their approach towards you. The three clear categorized behaviours that are most evident in human beings that we need to be able to recognize, identify, and adjust to suit the desired outcome of a potentially disastrous situation include the following:

Strong, over the top, pointing a finger, and intimidating

Alpha

Dominant, aggressive, lecturing, one-way communication, parent—we will call this group Alpha.

Sensible, open arms/hands when talking, gentle smile, eye contact, welcoming

Equal

Assertive, mediator, two-way communication, adult—we will call this group Equal.

Submissive body language, cowering down slightly and very agreeable

Submissive

Passive, accommodator, timid, submissive, very agreeable, sulky child; we will call this group Submissive.

The key here is if someone is being an aggressive alpha, their voice is raised. They point their finger at you, and their posture is stiff and framed in a threatening way. To prevent an alpha–alpha fallout would destroy the relationship as it may include physical fighting or no one winning. A victory is not given as there is no compromise. It is important to assume the submissive role in this type of situation initially as it will give the other party time for their temper to cool and also give you time to take a break and calculate what the next steps are. The next step may be to wait for the rage episode to subside then move yourself into an assertive adult, an equal mode, and this will hopefully, in turn, bring the lecturing parent or alpha into an assertive space, creating the desired form of healthy and productive behaviour and communication style.

Another scenario may be that a colleague or boss talks to you in a parental way, making you assume a submissive child position. To ensure this unhealthy behaviour or communication style is broken, the submissive child needs to move into the 'equal' adult status and bring the other person down from being an alpha parent to an equal two-way communicating adult.

Can I suggest you look at some of the relationships you have with friends, family, and colleagues, and begin to practice in real-life situations and see the change in your behaviour and theirs? The most fun I have had and a bigger challenge is to break down that lecturing parent-and-child relationship and bring both to an equal adult relationship. It is hard to demonstrate this when writing in a book, so I am hoping the illustrations will at least help you to identify the characteristics of such behavioural traits and types.

Chapter 6

Goal Setting and Navigating Our Path for Success

I am a firm believer that we can do anything we want as long as we set the pathway to success and put in the hard work while not losing sight of the goals we have set. In simple terms, a goal is something we want to achieve to create the success we want for the reason(s) we have chosen.

Goals can include being wealthy, having a great career, having an expensive motor vehicle, having a nice home, having great friends and relationships. Sure, we don't always get everything; however, in my experience, we can get very close, and it starts with setting goals that are focused and achievable. I wanted to have a house in a particular very expensive location and drive and own a new sports Mercedes. I wanted to be paid very well working in an executive role in an industry that helps people and makes a positive difference to many, not just a few. I wanted a son. I wanted to complete a master's degree and be recognized for my work achieved and that I and the teams I lead would be awarded. And actually, it did result in a gold medal nationally, a gold medal in the Asia Pacific region, and a bronze medal worldwide! In turn answering another goal of mine—ultimately allowing me to be an international speaker and able to see the world, all paid for! Oh, and also to be happy!

Coming from nothing, not able to get into university at the end of school and losing my way, to now be able to share these successes with many was another goal I wanted to achieve.

Where a lot of people get it wrong is they waste their energy on issues they cannot directly make an impact on at the time and place they are in. For example, world peace, war, global warming, and similar. It is important to remove the noise and focus on those goals, building blocks that are realistic and will deliver you happiness, and you will achieve what you want to achieve. As you climb the ladder to your personal success, each milestone, each rung in the ladder, is celebrated, acknowledged. The bigger global issues may come into the mix once the fundamental platform of your success is in place. We need to climb the rungs in the ladder of success before achieving the ultimate goals set. It is so important to celebrate milestones to enrich the process and formula to success.

Goals need to be seen and the work towards the goals observed, measured, and as achieved, celebrated. The ability to acknowledge each achievement along the way. Positive self-talk that this can and will be achieved, and a *can* versus *cannot-do* attitude is essential. Feeling sorry for oneself—'It is not fair, they have it and I don't'—will not work. Be thankful for what you have, and build from there. Risks may need to happen; for example, if you are in a job that is not allowing you to move forward, then move jobs, study more, and look at other ways of moving forward. If the environment is not right for you, surrounded by negative people and behaviour, to achieve your goals, you may have to make tough decisions and remove negative influences from your life as your energy needs to be focused on achieving your personal goals. Where possible, surround yourself with positive and successful role models.

Goals take work to achieve and a positive frame of mind that success can, will, and does occur for you. Others may try and send you different messages, and their intent may not be genuine. Believe in yourself, and others will believe in you. Create a circle of people that are also working to their goals and share positive stories and journeys together. There is an old saying: 'If you lie down with dogs, you will wake up with fleas.'

Chapter 7

Feedback and Mirroring: Adapting our Behaviour for Success

Constructive feedback to adapt your behaviour is positive; however, you should not change 'you' or the identity that makes you an individual and who you are and comfortable being. Use the feedback, research, and observations to be adaptive, like a chameleon changing your colours to suit the situation so to speak. This ability to be flexible and adaptive is an enabler for the goals that you have set for your pathway to personal happiness and success.

We have all heard the saying 'There is no *I* in team.' On the contrary, a team is a group of people working together to achieve a common purpose or goal. A successful team is one made up of committed individuals that are important in making a contribution and have the skill of adapting behaviour to blend in and influence other team members to move the purpose in the right direction. As an individual, you need to contribute and belong. To belong, we need to look at how others behave or even look like they do, i.e. clothing, demeanour, approach so that we can assimilate into this environment and become a valuable contributor and member of the team.

It has been documented through the decades about mirroring behaviour where one looks, acts, and behaves like someone else in essence to be accepted. I have practiced this in my career. If you have a role model that is successful in your eyes and many other eyes, then if this is aligned to your pathway, then mirroring is not a bad thing. For example, I wonder what X would do in this situation. How did X overcome this barrier? Understanding your role model and mirroring some of the behaviours is positive.

ANYONE CAN BE SUCCESSFUL

If you want to belong in an organization, team, or support group, then adapting your behaviour to suit the style, type, and mission of that team is essential. It is like when one is going for a job interview, research on what the culture is like. How do people dress? What does the client base expect? What do other employees and managers expect? What language do they use? And similar.

Charles Darwin said, 'It is not the fittest or smartest that survive, it is the ones most adaptable to change.'

Mirroring and adapting behaviour via constructive feedback is only a part of the techniques. To ensure the success is embedded, you need to

- visualize what it is you want,
- believe in it,
- live it, and
- become it.

Repeat this regularly, and it will become your DNA and reality.

This will become your reality. As we saw in goal setting, carefully plan the steps with observable, measurable timelines and milestones, celebrating along the way. Having visual messages such as a picture of the house you have always wanted or the job, car, career, successful role model, or similar on the fridge at home, on your desk at work or school, in your wallet or similar allows you to remember why you are doing the things you have in place to ensure success. It may also allow you to alter the path as you move along.

Constant reminders and repetition helps to fill our control centre (brain) with positive messages, and when repeated and believed, they will end up in our subconscious and, in turn, will become our beliefs and world view. The control centre (brain) will adapt our thinking to assimilate us into the person we want to be to enable the journey to success!

Chapter 8

Professional Athlete Approach to our Well-Being

Having moved into executive roles over the past decade, I have found myself using the success strategies in this book more regularly than ever before. The hours have got longer, the pay has got better, my control centre (brain) is growing, and I am becoming more adaptive and my goal setting has never been clearer. Also, my pathway to success has crossed off a lot of the rungs in the ladder and celebrated the milestones along the way.

Globally we celebrate athletes, and today, the Olympic Games still sustains one of the largest followings and viewing audiences in the world. Having worked with one of the most awarded female Olympians in history, I learnt a lot.

What I learnt was athletes at the top of their game have access to psychologists, dieticians, and therapy services such as massage, a coach, and so much more.

Not all of us have access to all these support services, so it is very important to know when we are becoming deflated and our balloons are at threat of becoming empty, and we allow too much stress in and are at threat of becoming distressed and unwell. Distress is harmful; stress is OK as it is a stimulus that keeps life interesting and us active. The issue is when there is too much stress and this transforms into distress.

This chapter will provide some helpful strategies on understanding why we need to say no when we are too busy, identifying triggers that change our behaviour to negative, understanding what happens when someone upsets us and our behaviour changes and we feel embarrassed as we have shown our true colours or responded to quickly and caused an adverse reaction, and understanding why our control centre (brain) did not back us up when we were pushed too far, preventing ourselves from responding adversely and knowing how to identify this. Finally, a quick look at diet, sleep, exercise, and finding ways to strengthen our soul, body, and mind for resilience.

The human body is very resilient, and when you are performing at your best, often you forget to take the time to ensure that there is always some energy and impetus in reserve. We need this energy in reserve so we can allow our control centre (brain) to think clearly and make the right decisions. When we are run down, we may not perform at our best. Recognising that the world will still function if you are not in it is important; prioritizing things that have to be done and ranking them in order of importance can assist in knowing what you may be able to put on hold and come back to later.

A good exercise when feeling overwhelmed and the vehicle's (body's) petrol tank, so to speak, is running on empty is to draw up two columns on a piece of paper. The tops of the two columns have the headings I Can and I Cannot.

If it is about more than one person making the decisions, such as your partner, a family member, or a close friend, then the headings may include We Can and We Cannot.

Under these headings, list the things that are worrying you and things that you feel you can and cannot change. The areas that fall into Cannot, leave for later or cross off your list for good. The things you can control and work on, then prioritize on a number scale of, say, 1 through 10, ranking the most important from immediate-, short-, middle-, and longer-term, and set time frames and goals—enablers to achieve. This exercise will help to balance the pressure you are under and make it more realistic and digestible to manage. You may like to leave the Can (prioritized list) on the fridge or at your desk at work as a reminder of the core areas to focus on and also cross them off as they are achieved. Also revisit this list from time to time as required to keep it up-to-date, relevant, and most of all, achievable.

Recognizing the signs that you are running out of energy is also important, such as aching joints, a sluggish feeling, poor response to other people, feeling tired, agitation, upset stomach, bags under the eyes, frustration, and finding it difficult to put the strategies discussed in this book into action.

When the 'fuel tank' is running below the 20 per cent mark and you have recognized this, then it is time to get this machine 'serviced' and back up and running. Between a broken-down old car and a Ferrari or Lamborghini, which you would prefer to be in for filling your success? Like a motor vehicle, our engine needs to be serviced, cared for, refuelled, and tuned up, so to speak. To ensure we do this, there are three main elements:

- Nutrition—fuel for the engine (body)
- Control centre (brain)—servicing and fine tuning
- Spiritual well-being (soul)—activities to make us feel good and happy

Nutrition (Body)

This is the absorption of nutrients from various food sources and how they interact with our bodies.

Nutritious foods that have high antioxidants, healthy nutritious factors for sustainable health and energy include fresh fruit and vegetables, and research shows that super foods include bananas, celery, kale, and berries—they are high on the list for good nutrients. Overall, a balanced low-fat diet is recommended and contains essential nutrient elements of carbohydrates, fat, fibre, protein, minerals, and trace minerals, vitamins, water, and salts.

For me to sustain a healthy balance, each morning I have a blended drink (nowadays there are many cheap and effective options for quick one-cup blending). This is fast and cheap, and the fruit and vegetables last the week. The ingredients I include are one carrot, one stick of celery, one kale leaf, one orange or mandarin, a handful of frozen mixed berries, and grape juice. This then allows me to eat other food without compromising my energy levels. It is OK to eat other food as long as there is a balance and can be likened to the fuels we can choose for a motor vehicle; for example, there is a difference between 'leaded fuel' (fatty food), 'unleaded fuel' (medium-nutrition quality food), and 'high-octane fuels' (highly nutritious food) for your motor vehicle. The great thing is in most cases, our high-octane fuels such as fruits and vegetables are the cheaper option!

Control Centre (Brain)

Did you know smiling and laughing have proven to have wonderful effects on the brain, body, and soul? The physical action of smiling (even if we are not happy) tells the brain that we are happy and releases endorphins that, in turn, increase the white blood cell count in our bodies (the white blood cells are what we use to fight disease).

If you smile a lot, you generally become happier and healthier. If you laugh a lot and even belly laugh, you do so much good for your brain, body, and soul as it refuels the positives and removes the negatives.

In essence, you need to find ways of making you smile, laugh, and laugh louder and bigger! I use happy places and people to help me with this. My happy places include associating with key people in my life, friends and family that make me laugh, also watching comedy shows that make me laugh, and spending time with my dog, who always makes me smile.

I also surround myself at home with visual reminders of happy places, such as past holidays, possessions that mean a lot to me, photos, and milestone achievements such as awards. These all remind me of self-worth and happiness and allow me to smile and feel safe and comfortable.

Your control centre is working hard for you on a daily basis, blocking the wrong messages, absorbing the right ones, recognizing and controlling how you behave and respond to various challenging situations and also keep up with the day-to-day challenges of life.

However, it also moulds us to reach and exceed our goals and set pathways. So as this control centre pumps over approximately five hundred words per minute, let's reward our control centre by remembering to smile, laugh, and increase our well-being through bringing in some positive feedback, a positive outlook, and happiness.

Even though sometimes it can feel as though we are living and working in a world of darkness being judged all the time, we need to sometimes be the candle that lights the way for ourselves and, in some cases, for others. If you are going to judge me, then you had better be perfect at what you are judging me about!

To find reasons for smiling and laughing, maybe too hard sometimes, remember even if you are not happy, the physical action of smiling and laughing will tell the control centre (brain) you are happy and release all the good fuels such as endorphins to set off some good oils such as white blood cells and ultimately build your resilience and set you back on the path to success!

I have sat at my desk when feeling unwell and smiled (made sure no one was looking, of course). When you get up in the morning, look in the mirror and practice smiling and laughing. It has also been proven that if you are a happy person or even give off the impressionthat you are happy (i.e. faking a smile), you will, in turn, attract positive people and responses. It has also been proven that if you laugh, laughter is contagious and others will laugh with you. I know I have found myself in a high-pressure situation and got the giggles, and others did as well! There are other areas that have been proven, so to back me up, I will share, and you can try these yourself. Just so you know, the smiling and laughter thing works, and I am not mad? Did you know if you are in a group situation where everyone is sitting down, if you yawn, others will follow? Did you know your foot is the size of your forearm (elbow to wrist)? Go on, I know you will try and measure this.

So to keep our control centre (brain) happy and well-rewarded, we need to absorb positive feedback through happy places and thoughts and also boost our body and soul with the power of smiling, laughing, and laughing louder! Happiness is important.

Spiritual Well-Being (Soul)

For our soul to be balanced, we need to exercise. This allows unwanted negative energy to be expended, and it also increases our blood flow and allows us to sweat out toxins, and also, we naturally feel much better due to the release of endorphins and additional white blood cells. Exercise is often seen as an inconvenience, and we tell ourselves that we are too busy. There are simple ways to remain balanced through exercise, and the best exercise is walking. This does not put too much pressure on the body and (unless disabled) is something we can do regularly by changing our habits. It has been proven that even thirty minutes a day will increase your well-being and health. Walk; don't take the car. Walk; don't take the lift. Take the stairs or a similar route.

Exercise is also good for strengthening our muscles, for healthy skin, for supporting our vital organs through better circulation, and for allowing our control centre (brain) to function at optimal capacity, in turn helping us to achieve our goals and enabling the success strategies covered in all chapters in this book!

Conclusion

It is so important to know who you are, how to be what you want to be, and how to look after yourself. Be self-aware and reward yourself along the way as goals and benchmarks are achieved. When you are in a good place and know how to sustain this and more, then your world will reward you, and in turn, you can help many more.

The key here is not to get lost and listen to the wrong messages and/or the wrong messengers.

To understand oneself and how to manage you is important; the rest will follow easier.

The perception of others is reality to them. You can always change others' perception of you when you have the craft of self-belief; the control centre (brain), behaviour, and communication management mastered; and the ability to carry out the functions highlighted in this book from deflecting the negatives, absorbing the positives, keeping your self-esteem and health in check, to mastering the elements of mirroring, prioritizing, goal setting, and effective behaviour management and communication techniques.

The power of you as an individual is amazing. There is so much negativity in the world. We cannot fix everything; however, if you can be the best at what you want in your life, then you will touch and help so many along the way. I hope this book has helped many as it has helped me. This book has been crystallized across over twenty years of academic study, motivational training, short courses, life experience, and working with disadvantaged people to some of the richest people in my country of origin, Australia.

This is a book to share the positive vibes and provide the tools to ensure your life is enriched. And know, at the end of the day, you are one person out of over seven billion in this world. So many people see difference as a disadvantage. In my life, success has come from bringing all sorts of people together—the melting pot of humanity—and working together and understanding the strengths each has to offer, and that difference in people is essentially the success factor. Drawing on your own strengths and goals and putting the enablers discussed in this book into practice and sharing these skills will certainly help you to reach your desired goals and, of course, help others along the way.

It will and does take hard work; however, once the routines and formulas are in place, then apply hard work and ensure to track your success as *effort* has to equal *results*! If the effort is not channelled to your goals, then readjust!

Remember to smile and laugh along the way. Life is short, so make the most of it, and I wish you all the very best at discovering who you are and how your control centre works, and finding some helpful hints and tools along the way to make you the best at what it is you want to be and do!

Thanks for taking the time to read this book, and I wish you every success in applying the new areas learnt or building on what you may have already known.

Onwards and upwards!

In good spirits,
Ben Oxford

Author Biography

Mr Ben Oxford (MEd, BProfSt, BTchg, Queen Elizabeth II Trust recipient, Queens Trust, Australia) has twenty years' experience in customer service and senior management across a number of sectors, including transport and logistics, gaming and entertainment, health and community, finance, mining, and the energy and utilities sector.

Ben Oxford's background is in building and enhancing customer engagement models for small, medium, and large enterprises. Significant achievements where outstanding results have been recognised were as national client services manager (finance sector) for three years, senior executive manager customer operations (health care sector) for three years, and most recently, his role as section head customer service (utilities sector) for two years in the largest interconnected and isolated electricity network in the world. The focus for these medium to large organisations was around simplification; centralisation to increase customer responsiveness; efficiency; customer attraction, acquisition, retention, and satisfaction; and accommodating growing volumes, sales, and complexity with scalability. These critical business elements increased benefits immensely, both for customers and staff, and for bottom-line results. The robust models were built around customer service levels, contact centres, CRM management, multimedia, balanced KPIs (big people and technology focus), 24 × 7 × 365 operations, record-keeping, and reporting. People, processes, and technology were all recognised independently at state, national, and international levels for excellence. The models directly affected over two million customers and had, at the time, great complexity across Perth Metropolitan, Regional Western Australia, and Australia.

The best practice experiences especially gained over the past decade have now culminated into his most recent role as executive chief, customer engagement for a large health care and retirement living provider.

Mr Ben Oxford has participated on boards for over a decade, holds three degrees including a master's in education (major in MBA leadership), and is a recognised international chairperson and keynote speaker at conferences and events across the country and globe from Perth to Singapore, London, Las Vegas, Sydney, and Melbourne. Over the past decade, Ben has and is currently a national (CSC) and international judge (CCW, EMEAS, APAC, and AMERICAs).

Recent customer service and operational excellence awards that Ben and the teams he has led have won include but are not limited to state, national, and international levels (ATA, MIAA-MPA, CSC, and CCW).

Some Career Highlights

- 2014—won Western Australia Best Marketing Content and Brand Revitalisation, Australian Marketing Institute of Australia (AMI)
- 2014—won Australia Best Customer Service, Information Communication Technology, Customer Service Council of Australia (CSC)

- 2014—won Customer Service Excellence, finalist, Customer Service Operations Centre, Australia, Australian Institute of Management (AIM)
- 2013—won Bright Spark Award for Making a Positive Difference
- 2013—National Customer Service Excellence Award for Outstanding Contribution to the Customer Service Industry, presented by the Right Honourable the Lord Mayor Lisa Scaffidi
- 2012—won bronze medal, Contact Centre World Awards Top Performers in the Contact Centre Industry (CCW); Best Medium-Sized Contact Centre in the World Award in Las Vegas, USA
- 2012—won gold medal, National Customer Service Excellence Award (medium), Customer Service Council (CSC)
- 2012—won gold medal, Contact Centre World Awards Top Performers in the Contact Centre Industry (CCW), Best Medium-Sized Contact Centre in APAC
- 2008—won bronze medal, Contact Centre World Awards Top Performers in the Contact Centre Industry (CCW), Best Medium-Sized Contact Centre in APAC
- 2007—won Australian Teleservices Association Excellence Awards (ATA), Best Medium Contact Centre in Western Australia
- 2007—won Customer Service Council Excellence Awards (CSC), Best in the West Outstanding Customer Service Excellence, large organisation category
- 2006—won Customer Service Council Excellence Awards (CSC), High Commendation for Customer Service Excellence
- 2004—won Australian Teleservices Association Excellence Awards (ATA), Best Small Contact Centre in Western Australia

- 2003—won Mortgage Industry Association of Australia Excellence Awards (MIAA), Best National Customer Contact Centre Operations
- 2002—recognised by Premier for Voluntary Board commitment with a medal
- 1997—recognised for Best Practice Placement program for long-term unemployed people, Jobs Australia
- 1994—recognised by the Queen's Trust of Australia for leadership

Index

A

action listening 28, 38
adrenaline 40
athletes 55

B

behaviour 20, 24, 26, 32, 35-6, 39, 42, 46, 48, 51-2, 54, 58, 67
 difficult 39
belief system 7, 14-17
brain 7, 15-19, 21, 23-5, 31, 35, 40, 42, 54-5, 58, 61-3, 65, 67

C

communication 11-12, 28-9, 31-3, 35-6, 38-9, 43-4, 46, 67, 70
 non-voice 28, 35-6, 38
 voice 28, 31, 35-6, 38
compliments 21, 24-5

conflict resolution 39
control centre 5, 15-19, 21, 23-5, 35, 54-5, 58, 61-3, 65, 67-8

D

deflection 21
differences 8
distress 19-20, 56

E

emotional connection 32-3
emotional state 19
endorphins 62-3, 65
energy 20-1, 32, 48, 58, 61-2, 65, 69
eye contact 29, 31, 38, 44

F

feedback 15, 20, 24-5, 31, 36, 38, 51, 54, 63

constructive 24, 36, 51, 54
  negative 15, 20, 24
fight-or-flight reaction 40
fuel tank 61

G

goal setting 17, 24-5, 39, 47-9, 51, 54-5, 58, 63, 65, 67-8

H

handshakes 29, 35-6
happiness 9, 15, 20, 48, 51, 62-3
happy places 62-3

I

image 29
impressions 29, 35
inflation 20-1, 25
influencers 16-17

M

messages:
  negative 25
  subconscious 28, 31
modes of behaviour:
  alpha 39, 43, 46
  equal 17, 36, 39, 44, 46, 68
  submissive 39, 45-6

N

negativity 68
nutrition 61-2

P

paraphrasing 28, 38
personality conflict 26
physical language 28-9, 35, 38
posture 20, 29, 33, 35, 40, 46
pressure 7, 40, 58, 65

R

reflection 20-1
reinforcement
  positive 38
  subconscious 38
relationships, professional 32
resilience 20, 25-6, 58, 63

S

self-awareness 36
self-belief 9, 18, 67
self-esteem 17-21, 24-5, 36, 67
self-perception 25
self-talk 20, 48
six Ps 21
stress 19-20, 56
support system 36

T

team 32, 48, 51-2, 54, 70

W

well-being 18, 20-1, 24, 36, 61, 63, 65
WIFM (what's in it for me?) 9, 32
work environment 24

Made in the USA
Columbia, SC
13 October 2023

24293135R00048